Tablecloth

From the Quilt in a Day Series

By Eleanor Burns

ISBN 0-922705-24-0

Copyright ©1991 by Eleanor Burns

First Printing January, 1991

Design and Layout Quilt in a Day Art Dept.

Photography by Wayne Norton

Published by Quilt in a Day

1955 Diamond Street, San Marcos, CA 92069   (619)436-8936

Printed in the United States of America

Blazing Star Tablecloth

The octagonal shaped Blazing Star Tablecloth is a perfect accent piece for complimenting any home decor. When covering a low round 24" diameter coffee table, the borders of the Blazing Star Tablecloth hang gracefully 5" from the floor. Round wooden tables 26" high and 20" in diameter can be purchased inexpensively, as well as ruffled cloth table skirts for under the tablecloth.

Diamonds begin with straight-of-the-grain strips sewn together and then are cut on the 45° angle or bias with a rotary cutter. These diamond strips are sewn into eight triangular shaped patchwork pieces that later become the octagonal shaped star. Even though this strip method replaces the original method of tediously cutting and sewing together individual diamonds, **the Blazing Star Tablecloth is a project best suited for experienced sewers.**

Fabric Selection

Choose 100% cottons 45" wide of the **same weight and weave.** Introducing a soft fabric among firmer ones results in a distorted star.

(Optional) Select lightweight bonded 100% polyester batting or 20% polyester/80% cotton for the inside of your tablecloth.

Color Selection of Eight Fabrics

Select two different color families that compliment each other. From each of these families, select four prints with a gradation from a light, to a medium, to a dark, and finally, to a very dark shade. In addition, vary the scales of your prints, as a large scaled multicolored print, a small scaled print, a medium scaled print, and one that appears as a solid from a distance.

Fabrics A to D, all from the same color family, make up the middle of the Blazing Star. When the tablecloth is placed on a round table, these colors lie on the top of the table. Fabric A, the very dark color, is positioned in the center of the star. Since the center point is one of the most difficult points to match, avoid a solid colored fabric that maximizes imperfect match points.

Fabrics D and E, lights from each of the families, create the transition from one color to the next. Choose either one of these for the optional backing fabric.

Fabrics E to H, the second color family, make up the outside edge, and hang over the rim of the table next to the borders. Fabric H, the second very dark color, is the outer points of the star, as well as the first border. Using the same fabric in this border minimizes points not perfectly trimmed.

Avoid stripes and directional prints.

Yardage and Cutting

Octagonal Shape   Approximate Finished Size: 64" Across Center / 59" Side to Side

Cut out swatches of fabric and paste them in place with a glue stick.

First Color Family

Fabric A/Center
Very Dark First Color
1/8 yard
Cut (1) 2 1/2" strip

Fabric B
Dark First Color
1/4 yard
Cut (2) 2 1/2" strips

Fabric C
Medium First Color
1/3 yard
Cut (3) 2 1/2" strips

Fabric D
Light First Color
3/8 yard
Cut (4) 2 1/2" strips

Second Color Family

Fabric E
Light Second Color
1/2 yard
Cut (5) 2 1/2" strips

Fabric F
Medium Second Color
1/2 yard
(6) 2 1/2" strips

Fabric G
Dark Second Color
5/8 yard
Cut (7) 2 1/2" strips

Fabric H/ Outermost Edge
Very Dark Second Color

3/4 yard
Cut (8) 2 1/2" strips

Cut border yardage separately from star yardage.

First Border	Fabric H	1/3 yard	Cut (4) 2 1/2" strips
*Second Border	Fabric D or E	1/2 yard	Cut (4) 3" strips
Third Border	Fabric C or F	1 yard	Cut (8) 3 1/2" x 29" strips
Fourth Border	Fabric A or B	1 yard	Cut (8) 4" x 29" strips
Backing (**Optional if Serging Tablecloth**)	Fabric D or E	3 1/2 yards	Cut (2) equal pieces
Lightweight Bonded Batting (**Optional**)		81" x 96"	

*Second Border Fabric must be a full 44" wide. If it is less than 44", purchase 1 yard and cut (8) 3" x 22" strips.

Paste-Up Page

Cut one 5/8" strip from each of your fabrics and cut them on the 45° angle into diamonds. Paste them in place with a glue stick to visualize how the gradation of the diamonds will look before you begin sewing.

One of Eight Triangles

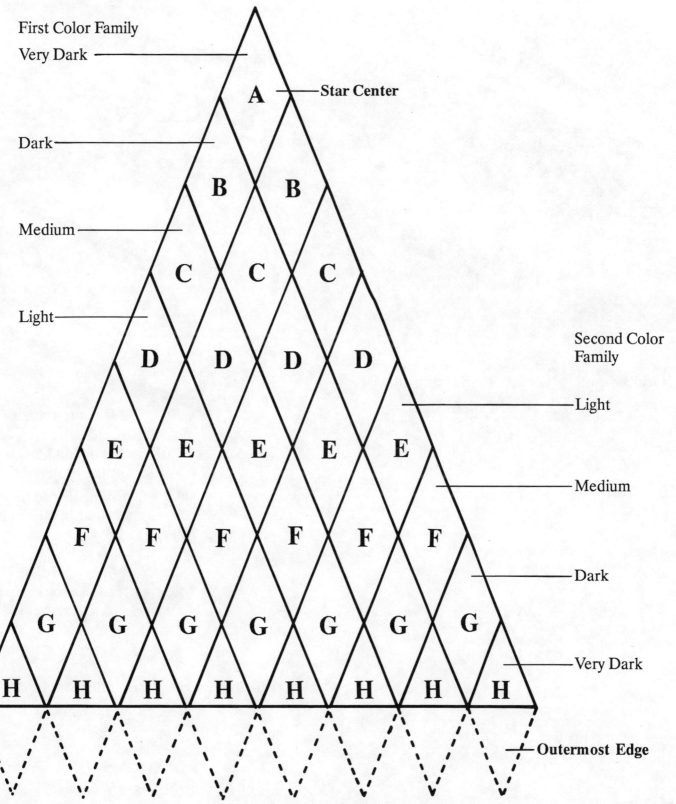

Supplies Needed

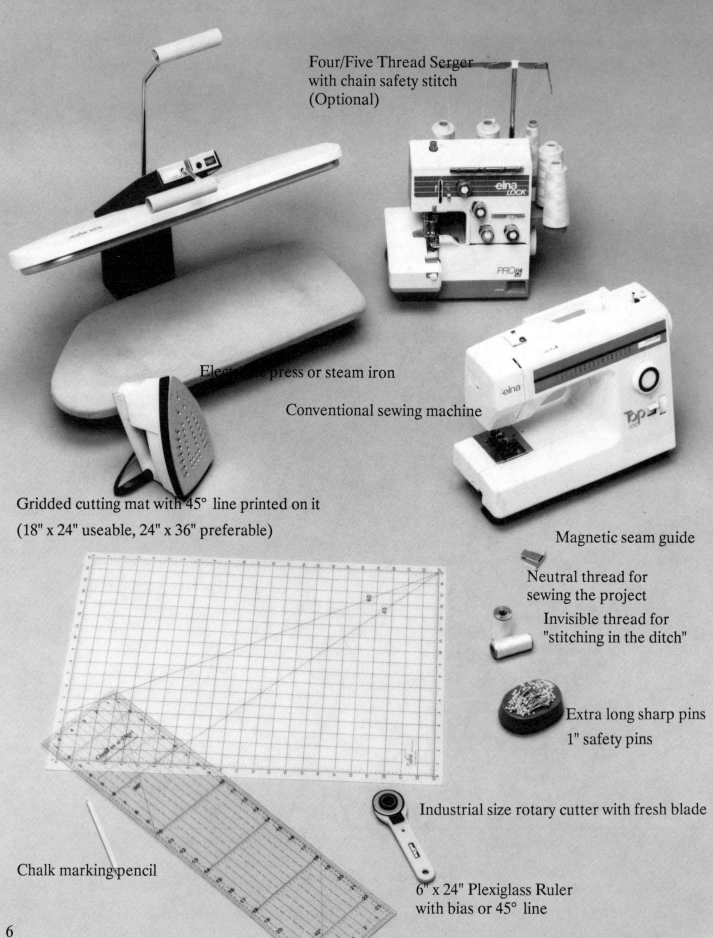

Four/Five Thread Serger
with chain safety stitch
(Optional)

Electric press or steam iron

Conventional sewing machine

Gridded cutting mat with 45° line printed on it
(18" x 24" useable, 24" x 36" preferable)

Magnetic seam guide

Neutral thread for
sewing the project

Invisible thread for
"stitching in the ditch"

Extra long sharp pins

1" safety pins

Industrial size rotary cutter with fresh blade

Chalk marking pencil

6" x 24" Plexiglass Ruler
with bias or 45° line

Cutting Star Strips

Refer to the Yardage and Cutting Chart on Page 4 for Number of Strips

Cut strips individually as described below, or **if you are confident in your cutting skills, you may layer cut** *to save time in the cutting process, as well as time when organizing your strips. Layer Fabrics A through D with Fabric D on the bottom. Straighten and cut a stack of strips 2 1/2" wide. Peel away and discard extra Fabric A as only one strip is needed. Place strip A 20" to the right of your sewing machine. Place strips B, C, and D to the left of A in reverse alphabetical order. After the second layered strips are cut, peel away extra Fabric B, as only two B strips are needed. Stack B, C, and D on top of the others. Repeat with Fabrics C and D, so there are three strips of C and four of D.*

Layer Fabrics E through H with Fabric H on the bottom. Straighten and cut five stacks of strips, and layer E, F, G, and H in order. Continue cutting, peeling away the top fabric, and restacking, so there are five strips of E, six of F, seven of G, and eight of H. See page 10 for strip layout.

Reverse this cutting procedure if you are left-handed.

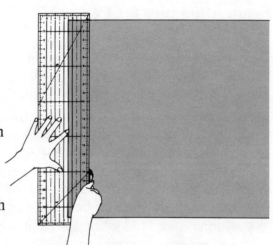

1. Make a nick on the edge of Fabric H and tear your fabric from selvage to selvage to put the fabric on the straight of the grain. Fold the fabric in half, matching the torn straight edge. It is often impossible to match the selvages.

2. Lay your fabric on the mat with most of it lying off to the right. Line up the quarter inch line on the ruler with the torn edge of the fabric on the left. Spread the fingers of your left hand to hold the ruler firmly. With the rotary cutter in your right hand, begin cutting with the blade off the fabric on the mat. Put all your strength into the rotary cutter as you cut away from you, and trim the torn, ragged edge.

3. Move the ruler over every 2 1/2", measuring and cutting the strips **carefully and accurately.**

4. Unfold and check to see that the strip is straight. If the strip is not straight, tear your fabric to put it on the straight-of-grain and begin again. **Cut all strips and stack in an H to A order to the right of your sewing machine. See page 10 for strip layout.**

Cutting Border Strips

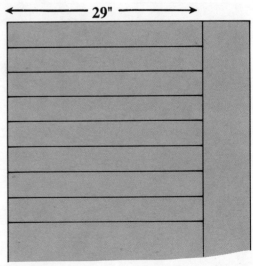

29"

1. The first and second border strips are approximately 45" long when unfolded.

2. On the third and fourth border fabrics, measure over 29", remove the remaining strip of fabric lengthwise and set aside for another project. After this lengthwise strip is removed, cut the widths of the border strips across the fabric.

Pointers to Help Your Star Shine

Conventional Sewing Machine Versus Serger

The entire tablecloth can be made with either a conventional sewing machine or serger. Both can be used if these two seam allowances can be matched thread to thread. The serger is faster to use when sewing strips together. Because of pin matching, the conventional sewing machine may be preferred when sewing diamonds together. The serger can be used again when adding borders.

If a completely serged tablecloth is finished without backing, the overcast seams should withstand machine washing.

Seam Allowance

Sew an accurate and consistent seam allowance approximately 1/4". This seam allowance must be used consistently throughout the sewing of the tablecloth.

Seam Allowance for Conventional Sewing Machine

The width of the presser foot usually determines the seam allowance. Line the edges of the fabric with the edge of the presser foot and sew a few stitches. Measure the seam allowance. If it is 1/4", a **magnetic seam guide** placed on the metal throat plate against the presser foot will assure a consistent 1/4" seam. If the measurement is less than 1/4", place the magnetic seam guide at a slight distance from the presser foot for a consistent 1/4". If the seam allowance measures more than 1/4", you may be able to adjust the needle position or feed the fabric so that it doesn't come to the edge of the presser foot.

Seam Allowance for Serger

If available, use the fabric guide attachment on the serger, and make the seam adjustment by moving the guide. Do not let the serger's knife trim the edges.

Conventional seam

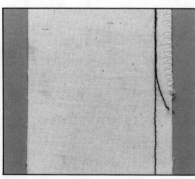
Matched seams

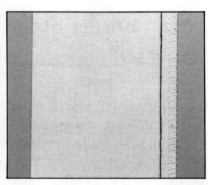
Serger seam

Strip Sewing

The strips must be sewn together in the left to right order as illustrated for each section. **Be careful not to pull on and stretch your strips as you sew them,** holding them together so they feed through the sewing machine at the same rate. Strips are always sewn right sides together.

Avoid Bowing in Sewn Strips

Bowing can be caused by using loosely woven, soft fabric, or when one fabric feeds faster than the other. Experiment by sewing two unpinned strips of the same fabric to see if one feeds faster than the other. You many have to adjust the thread tension and pressure on the presser foot or change how you hold and feed your strips.

Stitches Per Inch

Set your machine at a tight stitch, **15 stitches per inch,** or #2 to #2.5 on machines with stitch selections from #1 - #4. This small stitch is used because backstitching is rarely done.

Pressing

Using an electronic press or steam iron, **press gently** so strips and diamonds cut on the bias do not become distorted. Always **press across the strips** rather than down the length of the strips. Begin on the **wrong side first,** and press the seams to one side as directed. Flip the strips over and then press on the **right side. Make sure there are no folds at the seam lines.** If your sewn together strips "bow" slightly when they are laid flat, you may have stretched either when stitching or pressing. In that case, press again with steam and block them into straight lines. Press seams in the direction indicated as this is important to the overall method of construction.

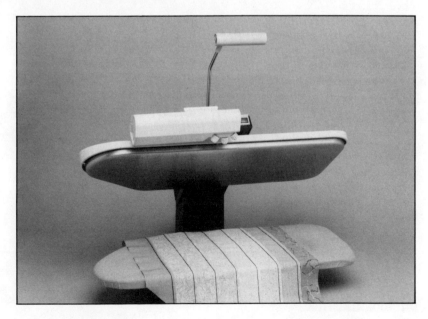

Press sewn together diamonds gently and sparingly so they do not become distorted.

Blazing Star Tablecloth

Strip Sewing Order

Making Section One

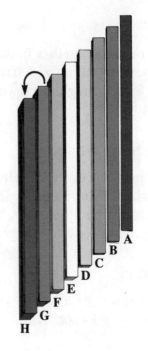

1. The 2 1/2" strips of each fabric are now lined up in this order. Work from left to right. Offset each strip 2".

2. Flip Fabric G onto Fabric H, right sides together, lengthwise. Position Fabric H two inches down from the top of Fabric G.

3. Sew with Fabric G on the top, wrong side up, and Fabric H underneath, 2" down from the top of Fabric G. Open.

4. Place Fabric F to Fabric H/G, right sides together. Position H/G 2" down from the top. Sew with Fabric F on the top of G, wrong side up. Open.

They should look like this.

5. Sew on the remaining Fabrics E, D, C, B, and A in the same staggered order.

10

6. **Press all the seams of Section One to one side away from Fabric H.**

   Turn right side up and press again. **Do not leave any folds at the seams.**

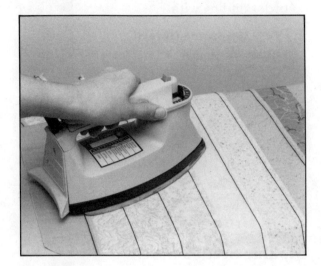 

In the remaining sections, the seams are pressed alternately toward and away from H.

Making Section Two

Section Two is sewn the same as Section One, ending with Fabric B.

1. Work from left to right. Offset each strip by 2".

2. Flip Fabric G to Fabric H, right sides together lengthwise.

3. Sew with Fabric G on the top, wrong side up, and Fabric H underneath, 2" down from the top of Fabric G.

4. Sew on all remaining strips in this staggered order.

5. **Press the seams toward Fabric H.**

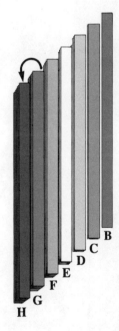

Making Section Three

1. Sew together one strip of each fabric in staggered order ending with Fabric C.

2. **Press the seams away from Fabric H.**

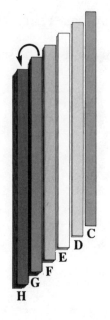

Making Section Four

1. Sew together one strip of each fabric in staggered order ending with D.

2. **Press the seams toward Fabric H.**

Making Section Five

1. Sew together one strip of each fabric in staggered order ending with E.

2. **Press the seams away from Fabric H.**

Making Section Six

1. Sew together one strip of each fabric in staggered order ending with F.

2. **Press the seams toward Fabric H.**

Making Section Seven

1. Sew together one strip of each fabric in staggered order ending with G.

2. **Press the seam away from Fabric H.**

Making Section Eight

1. Section Eight is only one strip of Fabric H. Sewing is not necessary.

Cutting Diamond Strips for the Tablecloth

1. Line up Section One on the gridded cutting mat with **Fabric H across the bottom.** Line up the seams so they are **parallel with the grid lines.**

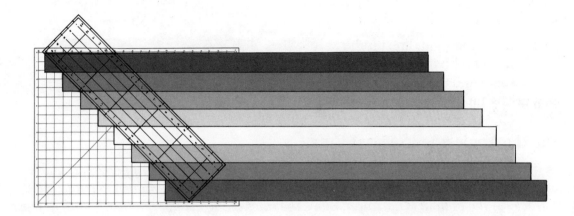

2. Find the bias line or **45° line** on the ruler.

3. Place the ruler's **45° line on the grid line above Section One** at the left end of the strip. Follow the illustration carefully.

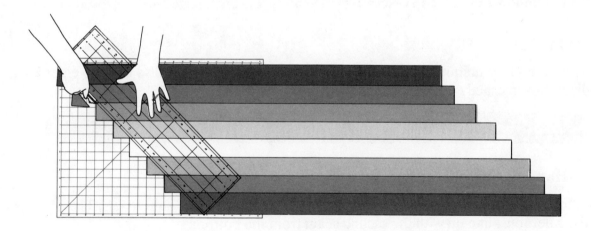

4. Trim off the left end on the 45° angle with the rotary cutter. This first cut is awkward unless you are left-handed.

   The easiest way to make this cut is to position the strip and ruler as illustrated, and then walk around the corner of the table and make the cut from the top down. Left-handed cutters: See bottom of next page to proceed.

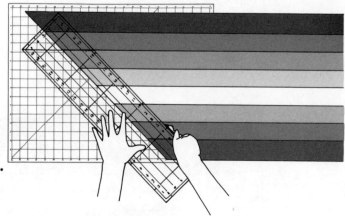

5. **Lift up and move** the ruler to the left until the ruler's **2 1/2" marks** are on the angled cut. Place the ruler's **45° line** on the second seam. Make sure that the 45° line is parallel with the lines on the gridded mat. Cut.

6. Lifting the ruler to the right, line up the ruler's 2 1/2" marks with the edge and 45° line with the seam and the gridded mat. **If necessary, gently tap the fabric into place. Cut.**

Correcting the Angle after Several Cuts

Bowed strips need correcting cuts. If the 45° line is on the seam and the upper 2 1/2" marks on the ruler line up with the cut edge, but the bottom is wider than 2 1/2", make the cut to put it back on track. If the bottom is narrower, move the ruler along the 45° line/seam until at least 2 1/2" of strip is under the ruler, and cut. Turn this diamond strip around, re-measure, and trim off the wider part.

7. Carefully and accurately cut a total of eight diamond strips 2 1/2" wide from Section One and from each of the remaining sewn sections with Fabric H across the bottom. Line up the 45° line on the ruler with the top seam. **Make sure that the 45° line is parallel with the grid.**

8. Cut additional Sections One and Two for practicing pin matching and sewing.

   Do not handle the cut strips excessively. Do not press until page 18.

Section Eight

Section Eight is unique because it is only one strip, Fabric H. It is also cut into eight 2 1/2" diamonds in exactly the same manner.

Left-Handed Cutters Only

After trimming the edge, turn the strips around and work from right to left. The 45° line on the ruler must line up with the second seam from the bottom.

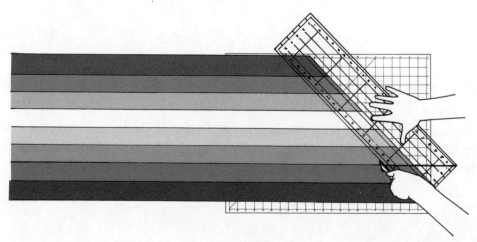

Arranging the Diamond Strips

The eight large triangles that form the star are each made of one diamond strip from each section.

Lay out the eight stacks of diamond strips in this order with Section One on the left and Section Eight on the right. **There are eight diamond strips in each stack.**

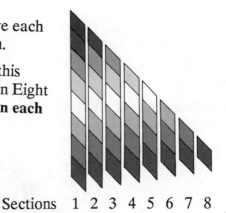

Sections 1 2 3 4 5 6 7 8

Matching and Pinning Diamond Strips

With this method of match pinning, you can continue using your magnetic seam guide or serger. Practice on your extra Sections One and Two.

1. Measure the seam allowance you have been sewing. It may be different from 1/4".

2. With your ruler and a pencil, draw dots at your identical seam allowance as shown on the wrong side of Section Two and the right side of Section One. When drawing the dot, back your ruler off just enough to allow for pencil lead width.

3. Position Section One and Section Two, right sides together, with the tip of Section Two approximately 3/8" above Section One.

4. Push a pin through the first match point on Section Two to the match point on Section One underneath. Be careful to pin through only one layer of fabric each time.

5. Stand the pin straight and pinch the layers of fabric together to keep them from shifting. Tilt and push the tip of the pin back through the fabric into the seam allowance.

6. Match all points with pins in this manner.

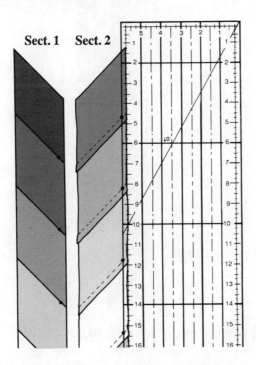

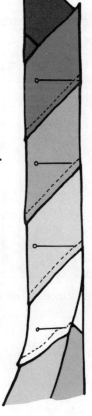

The dots represent the match points.

7. Sew this one set, pulling out each pin just before you sew over the match. Your needle and stitching line must cross the match point exactly.

You will damage your serger if the knife edge hits the pin.

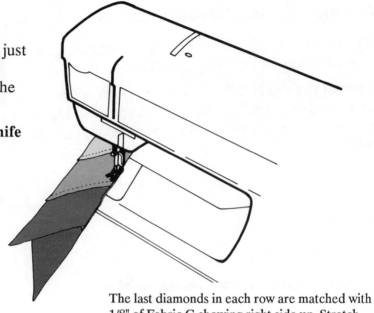

The last diamonds in each row are matched with 1/8" of Fabric G showing right side up. Stretch the top diamond, Fabric H, if necessary so that only 1/8" shows.

8. Check your matches from the right side. Check that the top outside edges line up. Check the match on the bottom diamonds.

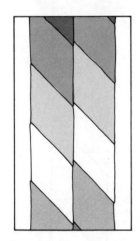

Seam allowance too narrow

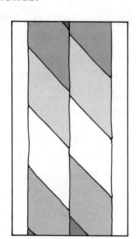

Seam allowance too wide

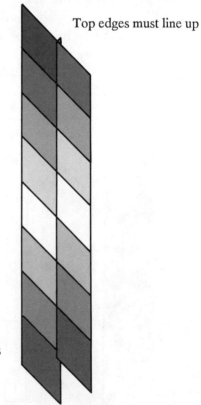

Top edges must line up

Check the match on the bottom diamonds

If you are not satisfied with the practice match or if the top edges do not line up, try again until you have mastered the technique.

Sewing the Diamond Strips into Triangles

The less you rip out seams, the less distorted the diamonds become.

Handle the diamond strips gently!

Make certain that the outside edges line up where the diamond strips are sewn together.

1. Match, pin, and sew Section One and Two together. Sew all eight sets together in assembly line order by butting and sewing one after the other, without raising the presser foot.

2. Clip the connecting threads.

3. Match, pin, and sew all eight diamond strips of Section Three to Sections Two.

4. Sew all diamond strips together in this manner.

5. Push the pin 1/4" in on the single H of Section Eight and match it to the seam in Section Seven.

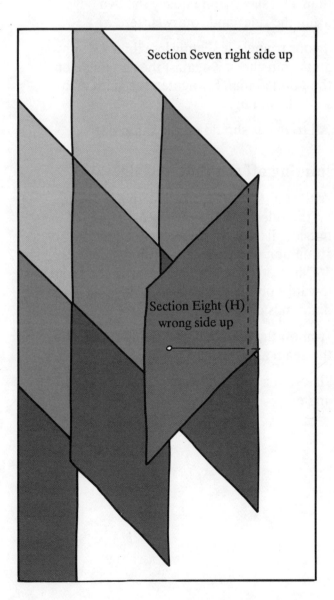

Section Seven right side up

Section Eight (H) wrong side up

Pressing the Triangles

1. From the wrong side, gently **press the seams away from Section One** toward Section Eight.

2. Gently press on the right side.

Checking the 45° Angle of Each Triangle

1. Lay the triangle on the gridded mat right side up, with the point of the triangle fitting into the 45° angle on the mat.

   Check to see that the outside edges line up. If the outside edge is uneven, a section may need to be unsewn, re-pinned, and sewn again.

2. If your triangle is equal to or slightly more than 45°, sliver trim equally the two edges using the ruler and rotary cutter.

3. If your triangle is slightly less than 45°, press, and again check it against the 45° angle on the gridded mat. Straighten the sides with sliver trimming.

   All triangles should be the same size.

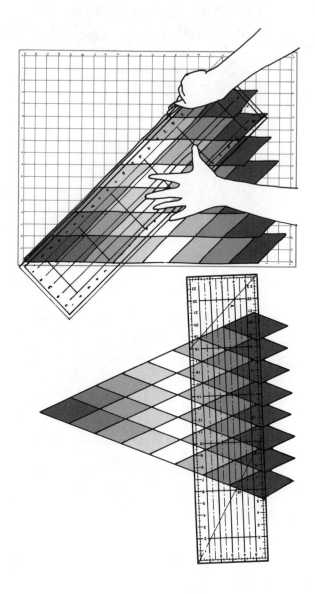

Trimming off the Bottom Edge

1. With your 6" x 24" ruler, line up the 1/4" line on the ruler with the outermost points of the outside diamonds. You may need to straighten underneath the ruler so that the 1/4" line on the ruler lines up with the seam allowance on the diamonds. Gently pull on the diamonds or large triangle.

2. Trim off the diamond tips, being sure to leave the seam allowance.

3. Place a pin in the bottom center of each triangle.

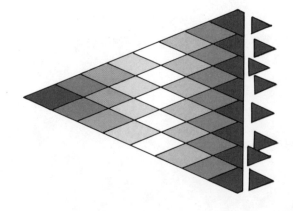

Adding Borders to the Triangles

1. Assembly-line sew the first and second border pieces together lengthwise.

2. Cut each piece in half so you have a total of eight pieces approximately 22" long. Fold in half lengthwise, and fingerpress in a crease at approximately 11".

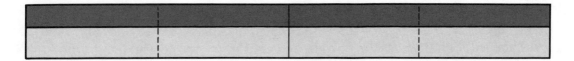

3. If you have not already done so, cut the third and fourth border strips into 29" lengths.

4. Piece together a third border strip and a fourth border strip until you have eight separate sections. Fold in half lengthwise, and fingerpress in a crease at approximately 14 1/2".

Optional Finish without Backing

Turn and press the raw edge under 1/4" on the fourth border. Turn and press under a second 1/4". Edgestitch this rolled hem with matching thread.

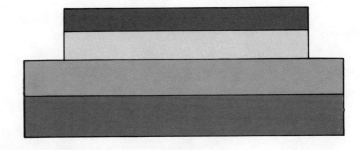

5. Piece together the eight first/second border sections to the third/fourth border sections, matching the creased centers.

6. Match the pin marked centers on the triangles to the creased border sections. Pin the center and outside edges.

7. Sew together with the diamonds on the top.

8. **Press the border seams toward the fourth border.**

Trimming the Borders

The borders are trimmed after two triangles are pinned together.

1. Right sides together, line up the right edges of two triangles with borders.

2. Pinch and wiggle the upper seams to interlock with the under seams. Pin along the seam.

3. Pin the center of the star and along the border seams.

4. Place the paired triangles on the gridded mat, with the pinned side on a grid line. Place the ruler on that grid line extending across the border, and continuing to the grid line beyond the border. This continues the 45° angle on the border sections. Cut this angle.

   Be careful not to undercut on the 45° angle, or the outside border edges will pull toward the center of the star, and it will not lie flat.

5. Repeat this pinning and trimming with the remaining triangles.

   Do not trim the borders on the second side until the triangles are pinned into halves.

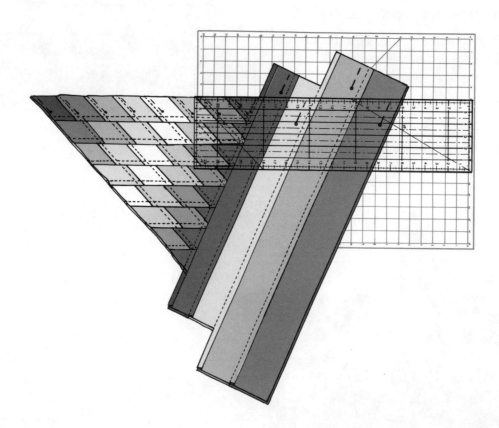

Sewing the Tablecloth Together

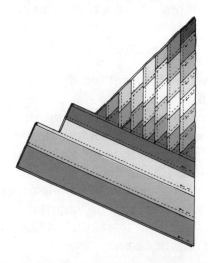

1. Lay out the pinned quarters.

2. Stitch all quarters from the center of the star to the outside border edge.

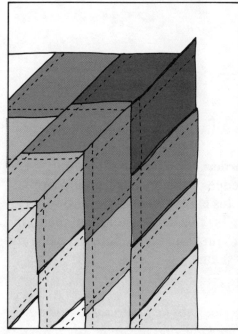

3. From the wrong side, gently press this seam to the left, clockwise.

4. Check the 90° angle by placing it right side up in a corner on the gridded mat. Sliver trim if necessary.

5. Trim off the tip from the seam allowance.

6. Pair the quarters and pin into halves along the right side. Trim the borders, and sew from the center to the borders.

7. Press the center flat. Sliver trim if the edge is not a straight line.

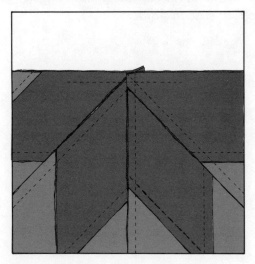

8. Pair the halves, and pin. Trim both borders.

9. Carefully match and pin the center point, pushing the seams in opposite directions. Sew across the center with 2" of basting stitch. Check to see if the center matches.

10. Sew the two halves together from the center to each side. Serger sewers may find it easier to sew from one outside edge to the other.

Checking the Tablecloth

Lay out the sewn together top on a large surface. If it does not lie flat, corrections can be made at this time.

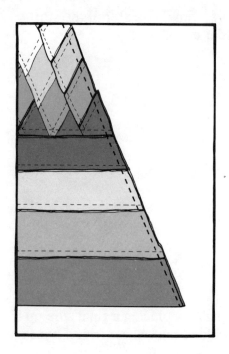

If the borders have been cut too short and are pulling toward the center, the star center tends to ripple. To correct this pulling, the seams in the borders can be let out. Beginning at the Fabric H diamonds, taper and sew the seam from 1/4" to 1/8" on the borders only, and remove the original 1/4" seam allowance. Try this adjustment on the four "quarter" seams first to see if the tablecloth lies flat before letting out the last four seams.

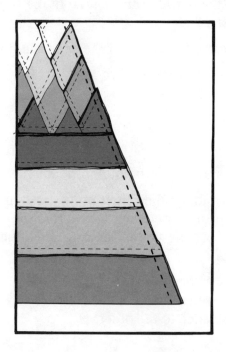

If the borders have been cut too long, the outside edge of the borders tend to ripple. Correct this excess by taking a 3/8" seam allowance. Try this deeper seam on the four "quarters" first and check before sewing the last four seams.

If the star does not lie flat, plan to add batting and backing, and finish by "stitching in the ditch" to ease in fullness.

Adding the Backing (Optional)

1. Cut the backing into two equal pieces.

2. Remove the selvages. Seam together lengthwise. Press the seams to one side.

3. Lay out the optional batting with backing on top, right side up on a large table or floor area.

4. Lay the tablecloth on the backing fabric with right sides together. Stretch and smooth out the top. Pin around the edges. Trim away excess fabric and batting so they are the same size.

5. Stitch around the outside edge, leaving a 12" opening in the middle of one side. Choose a side where the backing edge is on the straight of the grain rather than a bias edge.

6. Turn the tablecloth right side out. Smooth flat.

7. Handstitch the opening shut.

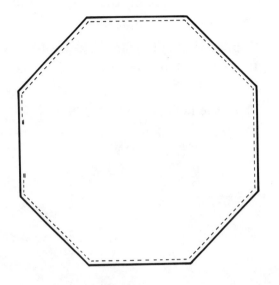

Safety Pinning the Layers Together

1. Plan where you will "stitch in the ditch" (stitch in the depth of the seam from the right side). Stitch as little as 12" across the center and around the first border, or as much as around each diamond row and border. Excessive fullness can be eased in with extensive machine quilting.

2. With 1" safety pins, pin-baste the layers together, beginning in the center of the star and working to the outside edges. Do not pin near seams that will be "stitched in the ditch."

3. Space your pins about every 5", pinning down the diamonds and the borders to be stitched.

   Pinning can be done quickly and easily with the use of a grapefruit spoon. Regular spoons can be used, but the serrated edge of the grapefruit spoon assists in closing the pin.

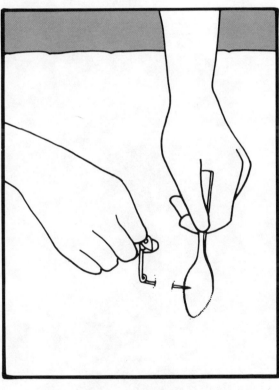

   Grasp the opened pin in your right hand and the grapefruit spoon in your left hand. Push the pin through the three layers, and bring the tip of the pin back out. Just as the tip of the pin surfaces, catch the tip in the serrated edge of the spoon, twist the side of the spoon up while pushing down on the pin, closing it.

4. You can also pin with straight pins. Pin "across the ditch" on the seams you wish to machine quilt. Pin the seams from the center out.

Stitching in the Ditch

To hold the backing and tablecloth together, "stitch in the ditch" with invisible thread.

1. Change your stitch length to 10 stitches per inch. Match your bobbin color of thread to your backing. Use invisible thread in the top of the sewing machine, and loosen the top tension.

2. Place the needle in the depth of the seam and stitch from the center outward. To avoid puckering on the back, use an even-feed foot or walking foot available for most sewing machines.